CATCHING MIST IN THE WIND

haikus by

Kenneth Francis Pearson

SCARMORA PRESS

To Walter Cummins & Renée Ashley

"Haiku is not a shriek, a howl, a sigh, or a yawn;
rather, it is the deep breath of life."
- Santoka Taneda

CATCHING MIST IN THE WIND

Scarmora Press
17630 South Bronze Mountain Pass
Vail, AZ 85641

First Edition
Printed in the United States of America
ISBN: 978-0-9768543-1-9

I.

"Toward those short trees
we saw a hawk descending
on a day in spring."
-Masaoka Shiki

Silent walk-through woods
is poetry – connection
is enlightenment.

Recognizing words,
wandering the path in verse,
poems dance in sky.

We are all poets,
who hear the universe cry –
through songs of nature.

Coyote journeys
through desert sand – existence,
is scattered by wind.

If only life, were
the heartbeat of hummingbirds –
a steady flutter.

Spotted ladybug,
exposes her wings to soar –
a meaningful flight.

Falcon soars through sky,
tips of feathers embrace breeze –
one with wind – with earth.

At night, screeching hawk
announces intent – the same
scream for land or love.

Springtime love flutters,
birds sing for the attention
of lifelong partners.

The eyes of the hawk,
searching for life's nourishment –
the phoenix rising.

Fly, fly mourning bird,
from ash tree – no sound, no words –
you, not unnoticed.

Listen to her sing,
through the dew of morning fog –
world lit like lamp light.

Perched is the falcon,
scanning barren desert land –
Quiet rabbit feasts.

Hummingbird wing song,
like the reverberating
murmur of a dream.

II.

"From time to time
the clouds give rest
to the moon-beholders."
- Matsuo Bashō

Eye's infinite views –
the moon inspires love and peace,
nature is content.

Litter in the night,
satellites orbit the earth,
eyes turned to the ground.

Oftentimes I feel,
like I am not meant for earth –
distant stars beckon.

Finite stardust eyes,
hum in harmony with night —
crooning melody.

Clouds drift silently
across distant horizon —
mountain peaks embraced.

In the dawn of day,
sunrise splits the horizon —
Venus radiates.

Time, space and mankind,
glide across the universe —
evolution looms.

Sun on horizon —
a still, singular moment,
triumph in presence.

Lonesome shooting star,
travels the vast universe —
a fleeting moment.

Distant galaxies,
forever unreachable –
youthful, naïve hearts.

Return to the earth,
the permanence of darkness –
penultimate black.

Universe vortex,
disintegration of stars,
drifts through dark matter.

The galaxy spins,
like violent cavalcade —
planets dodging death.

Clouds prance through night sky —
city glow illuminates —
radiating moon.

Moon's battered surface,
worn like a battlefield scar —
serves to warn mankind.

Early morning sun,
extends her arms and touches
the whispering dew.

Alas! Shooting star
over desert in winter –
Silent owl gliding.

The changing of guards,
as dusk overcomes the day –
moon and sun collide.

A touch of orange,
in a sky of white and blue –
Disappears the day.

In the great expanse,
we drift into nothingness –
Yet we still exist.

Cotton covered sky,
soft breeze and the threat of sun –
Earth with open arms.

Good morning, blue sky —
petrichor of summer's rain —
storm clouds drift away.

The sky elongates —
the foothills beg for mercy,
so too yearns my heart.

I gaze at night sky —
the infinite universe —
and search for meaning.

I prefer the night,
where the stars wink and whisper —
dreams, the shooting stars.

Stars on black canvas,
tiny gems, light years away —
beacon for fireflies.

Sadness — to succumb
to thoughts galaxies away —
in arms of lover.

III.

"Over the wintry
forest, winds howl in rage
with no leaves to blow."
-Natsume Sōseki

The prick of a thorn,
purity of nature scathed,
white petals blooming.

Sprouts the spring seedling,
from emergence to bare branch —
hollow winter tree.

Lovers entangled,
and even if lust should last,
a dying white rose.

Hickory leaves swirl,
on a path near pecan groves —
weary trimmed branches.

Trees sway in calm breeze,
sunlight dances with shadows —
youthful songbird sings.

Melodious as
wind through fallen hollow tree —
a still, peaceful death.

Snowflakes rest on limbs,
of outstretched maple branches –
Silence in echoes.

Willow tree weeping –
the tears of the world flow through –
birds sing soft sorrow.

The earth's mantle shifts –
bonsai tree on mountainside,
forever unmoved.

Like graceful dancer,
her petals tango with wind —
love waits to blossom.

Cherry blossom tree,
scatters pink on earth's green floor —
a blanket of hope.

A flower withers,
decaying ash falls to earth —
cycles to rebirth.

Tree stands quietly,
watching lonely passersby –
outstretched arms in bloom.

A frozen raindrop,
rests on stem of winter rose –
smoothed ice covers thorn.

Petals drift slowly,
circling through clean, springtime air –
soft touch of fingers.

Sun shines through branches,
weeping of the willow tree —
light casting shadows.

Fireflies shine at dusk,
rose petals littered beneath
feet — a lover's stroll.

Long blades of grass dance,
the waltz of an autumn breeze —
your long, flowing hair.

Reflecting shadows,
as I sit on the back porch —
thunder, and your hand.

Sun rays upon bank,
river reflects green pasture —
moments without you.

IV.

"The distant mountain
catches the sun.
The desolate field."
- Takahama Kyoshi

A desert voice heard,
wind through needles – saguaros
speak in native tongue.

Moments on rock ledge,
on stones, one billion years old –
a lonesome cloud rests.

Valley of colors,
of rainbows and wildflowers,
blanket untouched earth.

Autumn foliage,
colors cover the cold earth –
beauty before death.

Mist creeps through valley,
on a snail's journey back home –
dew before sunrise.

It is the silence
which rustles across wheat fields –
solitude smiling.

Observe and study,
the smallest of mountain rocks,
overlooking range.

Calls from the mountain –
I dreamt of the highest peak,
as I stood on clouds.

A creosote breeze,
touches distant memories,
a mind filled with past.

A symphony of
nature, tells story like wind,
through bamboo forest.

I am the desert,
my heart its relentless scape,
my love – its sunset.

Sun setting behind
distant horizon storm clouds –
pacific lightning.

Fog blankets valley,
mountains ascending from earth,
sun's hand touching peaks.

Moss covered forest,
left undisturbed by mankind –
a sparrow nesting.

Waiting at trailhead,
with unknown destination,
heart guided by life.

Shadows of clouds cast,
on yonder hills and valleys —
vultures' death circle.

Wind glides through valley,
touching leaves and wildflowers —
the sway of hammock.

Sleeping woodpecker,
saguaro arms praising moon,
a cool desert floor.

Singular moment,
when the sun breaks horizon –
I cry joyous tears.

Grand Canyon morning,
river snakes through layered stone,
translucent sunset.

Winter's weight of white,
bends branches in reverence –
reflection in stream.

V.

"Winter seclusion –
Listening, that evening,
to the rain in the mountain."
-Kobayashi Issa

Beneath river flow,
sun reflects smoothed granite stone,
once a jagged rock.

Water pools below,
the misting spray from rapids –
chaos in beauty.

Movement of water,
trickles like wind through branches –
a still photograph.

Like glass covered lake,
the sky soars in parallels,
faint ripple from stone.

Rain patters on sill,
like tapping of the snare drum —
lonely cries echo.

Trickles on my skin,
raindrops fall from clouded sky,
a burst of sunlight.

Snow on mountain peak,
sun transforms into liquid —
dry desert awaits.

The prattle of rain,
puddles pool on empty streets —
She sits by embers.

Waterfall cascades,
into swirling pools below —
a soaring eagle.

Ripples of water,
bridging distance between us,
connected by sea.

Tiny ocean wave,
ends its journey on the shore —
feet rooted in sand.

Clouds reflect on glass,
basking in still lake surface,
breeze rustles branches.

White water rapids,
a stream beneath rooted feet —
home is solitude.

The sound of water,
echoes off trees in forest —
mist catching the wind.

Cold is the ocean,
waves crash over tiny feet,
toes rooted in sand.

Sea water dances,
sun reflects off ocean waves,
horizon clouds drift.

I am pebbled sand,
riding the ocean current,
time sifts through hourglass.

Clear crystal water,
a palm tree bends in respect —
footprints washed away.

A seagull squawking,
a wave crashes against shore –
time does not exist.

Love lost in shadows –
a single leaf floats downstream –
waterfall teardrops.

VI.

"I write, erase, rewrite
erase again, and then
a poppy blooms."
- Katsushika Hokusai

I wish to live free,
where sun touches horizon,
and birds journey home.

Her adorned beauty,
season's ceremonial
spectacle of hope.

When I was a child,
I heard the soul of nature,
echo in my dreams.

When our journey ends,
we'll walk the world embracing
earth's impermanence.

One day I shall die,
somewhere in the mourning dawn,
the rose petals bloom.

Thank you for reading!

A LETTER FROM THE AUTHOR

Dear Reader,

The poems contained within this book were never intended to grow
into what they have. What started as three poem entrance into a poetry
writing competition, quickly grew into a daily reflection and reminder for
me to connect with nature.

This world has felt chaotic. People fighting over the most trivial of things
and lacking one of the most basic human functions - respect for others.

Writing poetry, specifically haiku, has been my solace from this chaos and
anger - a reminder that not everything in the world is ugly. It has been a
chance for me to disconnect and find comfort in the exploration of words.
Writing this book brought me closer to nature, closer to my family, and
closer to the things that truly matter to me.

If you feel lost or overwhelmed by the world, I hope you can find something that centers you - a book, a hobby, a passion - something that
brings you closer to the things that really matter in your life. I hope you
find yours like I have had the good fortune of finding mine. If you haven't,
keep searching. It is there waiting for your discovery.

As always, I want to thank you for reading and taking the time to catch a
small glimpse into my life!

With hopes for balance,
Kenneth

ACKNOWLEDGEMENTS

First and foremost, I would like to thank my wife, Cory Lynn Pearson, for supporting me. It is because of her that I am motivated to share my work with the world.

Thank you to my dog, Kiera, for acting as an alarm clock and waking me at 5:00am every morning with a soft whimper - reminding me it was time for her morning walk. I wasn't always happy about it, but I was always appreciative after the fact.

I would like to thank and dedicate this book to two incredible mentors - Walter Cummins and Renée Ashley - both of whom have impacted and inspired thousands of aspiring authors and poets. It is because of their willingness to share their expertise that their legacy will continue to live as so many will continue pass on this wisdom from generation to generation.

I would like to thank The Downtown Tucson Partnership and the University of Arizona Poetry Center for hosting their annual Haiku Hike Literary Competition. Without this competition, my exploration of haiku may never have become a reality.

A huge thank you to you, the reader. By supporting me, you support the dream of all Indie Authors.

Finally, to my family and friends, I want to thank you for your unwavering support. You have walked with me through every stage of my life and I could not have become the person I am without you.

ACKNOWLEDGMENTS

CONTACT
E-Mail Kenneth at kfpears@gmail.com

***

FOLLOW KENNETH ON SOCIAL MEDIA
Instagram: @kennethfrancispearson

***

Visit Kenneth's website at:
www.kfpearson.com

***

Lastly, Kenneth would appreciate your review of the book!

Kindly leave a review on Goodreads, Amazon, Barnes & Noble, Target, or wherever you choose to shop!

CPSIA information can be obtained
at www.ICGtesting.com
Printed in the USA
BVHW050205090223
658191BV00031B/1028